What peopl
Nadine Wel

CW00395075

"I have known Nadine ⸻ ⸻ ⸻ half years, as my French teacher. She has an excellent comprehension of the English language and a passion for her own mother tongue. The faux pas made by native English speakers when they try to communicate in French must be a rich source of humour, as well as being highly educational. I wish Nadine the very best of luck with her latest foray into the world of literature." – **Kim Potter**

"I have been attending Nadine's French conversation classes for several years. She is an excellent teacher and her understanding of the differences and similarities between English and French is extremely good. Our attempts to master the nuances of the French language must be very entertaining. Nadine's experience of teaching French to the English has resulted in a book that will be very useful and educational to anybody wanting to improve their knowledge and understanding of French." – **Tresanna Borgman**

Pour Guy

Nadine

Ah! Mais oui!

The fun way to learn French as the locals speak it – so you get what you want with a smile on your face

Nadine Webb

Did you spot the Eiffel Tower?

Contents

Thank you!

I would like to personally and warmly thank all my students, who have been the inspiration for this book.

Together we have encountered easy and difficult moments, talked, laughed and shared a lot.

They have accepted my very French way of approaching things, whilst combining English references – for example, saying that some mistakes are cute while others will make you sound like a complete pillock.

About the author

Nadine Webb is a French native from Normandy and has been a French teacher in Great Britain since 2003. In 2010, she decided to become a private tutor instead of working in schools as she preferred the personal approach and wanted to really mould her teaching to her students' specific needs.

Ever since then, she has been compiling notes about all the little difficulties that annoy learners and that you can rarely find in books, giving her the push to put them together in a book. Besides this, she wanted to add something a bit more fun, so she has explained the many idioms that are used on a daily basis, which will help any person living amongst French people to understand them or to use them too.

Bonne lecture!

How to use this book

- Try to read one page a day.

- Speak the words out loud in front of a mirror.

- Put a smiley face next to the expressions you love and want to use a lot in conversation, such as "**A tes souhaits!**" (Bless you!).

- Practice expressions with a friend.

- Email me at frenchtuition@gmx.co.uk if you have questions.

1

How to pronounce correctly so as not to sound like a fool

➢ Link words finishing with an 's', a 'x', or a 'z' with a word starting with a vowel or an 'h'.

For example: **des amis** (*dezamee*) or
vous habitez (*vouzabité*).

This also helps you breathe better and your language will flow.

➢ When you use **tout** in singular, you don't pronounce the last 't'. However, when you use **tous** (plural), you pronounce the 's' if it is not followed by a word.

In the phrase **tous les jours** you don't pronounce the 's'.

However, if **tous** finishes a sentence, you pronounce the 's': **Nous y allons tous** or **Nous en voulons tous**.

➢ When you use **plus** in a positive sentence, such as **Je veux plus de salade** or **J'en veux plus**, you pronounce the 's'.

However, if you use it in a negative sentence, such as **Je ne veux plus de salade** (I don't want more salad) or **Je n'en veux plus**, you don't pronounce the 's'.

➢ In most words that finish with a consonant, you don't pronounce the consonant.

i.e. **dans** – **beaucoup** – **et** – **blanc** – **jus** – **temps** – **nos** – **vos** – **trot** – **trop** – **croc**...

The exception is if these words are followed by a word starting with a vowel or an 'h', such as **vos amis**, **dans une heure** or **nos hôtels**.

➢ In colour adjectives such as **blanc**, **vert** and **gris**, the last consonant will only be pronounced when you form the feminine adjective: **blanche**, **verte**, **violette**, **grise**.

SO PLEASE NO MORE PRONOUNCING, EVER, THE 'C' in **un vin blanc** or **le Mont Blanc**.

Exceptions

➤ When a verb finishing in 't' is followed by 'à', you don't link them together.

For example:

Un balai sert à faire le ménage.

➤ Nord Ouest or Nord Est (not linked)

But: **Sud Ouest** or **Sud Est** (link the two words).

➤ The same applies when a verb finishing in 't' is followed by **et**.

For example: **Le chien part et le chat reste**.

➤ An egg: **un oeuf** (phonetic: *un neuf*).

Eggs: **des oeufs** (phonetic: *des zeu*).

➢ If you say **sans** (without), you don't pronounce the 's' if it is not followed by a vowel or an 'h', but if you say **sens** (meaning or sense), you pronounce the last 's'.

Examples:

Il parle sans arrêt.
Mais elle part sans beaucoup de bagages.
Ce que tu dis n'a pas de sens.

➢ Possessive adjectives: Please note that if a feminine word starts with a vowel or an 'h', you have to use the masculine version of the possessive adjective.

Examples:

mon amie
mon habitation…

2

Typically French traditions and unusual use of certain words

➢ When a woman has reached 25 years old and is not married, we say **elle coiffe la Sainte Catherine**. (This is rather an antiquated tradition now.)

➢ **C'est réglé comme du papier à musique**: It's working like clockwork.

➢ **La fenêtre donne sur le jardin**: The window opens onto the garden.

➤ **Je suis dans le train**: I am on the train.

➤ **un corbeau**: a raven.

Other usage: **Le corbeau a envoyé une lettre à la police**. This means, "An anonymous informer sent a letter to the police."

3

A few differences between French in Quebec and in France

Quebec	France
Souliers	Chaussures
Ma blonde	Ma petite copine *or* ma petite amie
Mon chum	Mon petit copain *or* mon petit ami
Faire du magasinage	Faire des courses
Tomber en amour	Tomber amoureux
Avoir du fun	S'amuser

4

Words adopted from other languages but used in everyday life

From Arabic

avoir la baraka: to be lucky

un bled: a village

le caïd: the boss

une casbah (ou kasbah): a house, a place

c'est pas bésef (ou bézef): it's not a lot

un chouïa (ou chouia, chouya): a bit

un clebs: a mutt

faire fissa: to be quick

faire la nouba: to have a party all night, to live it up

le flouze (ou flouse): dough (money)

un gourbi: a hovel

kif-kif, pareil: the same

Kif-kif bourricot: It is the same thing

macache: no way, not a chance

un ramdam: a racket (noise)

la smala: the tribe (family)

le souk (c'est le souk): the mess (it's a mess)

un toubib: a doctor

tout son barda: all his stuff

une veranda: a conservatory

From English

l'after-shave

l'airbag

ASAP

le babyfoot: table football

le/la baby-sitter

le bachelor

le banana split

le barbecue

la barmaid

le barman

le basket: basketball

la basket: the sports shoe

le bazooka

le bermuda: long shorts

le best-of

le bestseller

le big-up

la blacklist

le blackout

le blazer

le blockbuster

le blues (music or sadness)

le bluff

bluffer: to bluff

le bobsleigh

le bodybuilding

booké: booked

boom

le boss

le booster

b-to-b (business-to-business)

le bouledogue: the bulldog

le bowling

le box-office

le boycott

boycotter: to boycott

le brainstorming

le break

le breakfast

le briefing/debriefing

le brunch

le bug

le building

le bulldozer

le business

le businessman

le business model

le business plan

le buzz

le cameraman

le camping: the campsite

le cardigan

le cashflow

le casting (actors)

le challenge

le charter (transport aérien): the charter flight

le chat: the cat

checker ses mails: to check one's e-mail

le checklist

le chewing-gum

la city

le cloud

le clown

le club

le coach

le coaching

le cocktail

cool

le come-back

le corner

le cowboy

le crash

customiser: to customise

le cutter: the knife, cutter

le dancing: the dance hall

le dance floor

la deadline

le deal

le debriefing

le design

design: designed

le discount

dispatcher: to dispatch

DJ

downloader: to download

le dressing: the dressing room, built-in closet

dribbler: to dribble (sport)

le drive-in

le drive

le drugstore

l'email

exit

faire le forcing: to put pressure on something or someone

le fair-play

le fan (of a sport, a celebrity etc)

la fantasy

la fashion

le fast food

le feeling

le ferry

les feux de warning: the warning indicators

le flash-back

la flash-mob

le flirt

le flyer

les followers

le football

freelance

le fun

la girl

le gloss: lip gloss

le goal

le gospel

le gun

le hamburger

handball

happy hour

le hardware

high-tech

la hype

le hit-parade

le hold-up

le hooligan

la hotline

l'interview

le jackpot

le jean: jeans, denim

le jetlag

la jetset

le job

le jogging

le ketchup

le kidnapping

le kit

le knock-out (KO)

le lag

le laptop

le laser

le leader

le leadership

la life

le lifestyle

le lift

le lifting: the facelift

le living-room

le lobby

low-cost

le management

le manager

le marketing

le marshmallow

Master

le match

le meeting

le microphone

Miss

le music-hall

le night-club

non-stop

offshore

OK

open bar

le pacemaker

le parking: the car park

le patchwork

people: celebrity

le pickpocket

le pickup

le pipeline

le pitch

le plaid

le planning: the planning, schedule

le playback

la playlist

la pop (music)

le pop-corn

le post

le poster

le pub

quick

rebooter: to reboot

le revolver

le rush

le sandwich

le shooting: the photoshoot, film shooting

le scoop (news, media)

le shopping

le screenshot

le self-service

le sex shop

sexy

le show

le sitcom

le sketch (film/drama)

slow (dance, motion)

le smartphone

le smoking: the tuxedo

le snack

le sniper

le speech

speed

le sponsor

le squatteur: the squatter

le start up

le steak

le sticker

le stop: the brake, hitchhiking, stop sign, full stop

le strip-tease

le supporter

le talkie-walkie: the walkie-talkie

le talk-show

le thriller

le toast

le toaster

top (adj)

tuning

underground

vintage

le Web

le weekend

le workshop or **l'atelier** (n, *m*)

le zoo

le **zoom**

5

Words that sound the same but mean something completely different

French into English

➢ **Le ver vert va vers le verre** means:

The green worm goes towards the glass.

le ver: the worm
vert: green
vers: towards
le verre: the glass

➢ **une boite:** a box

un box: a horse carriage

➢ **jurer:** to swear (on the Bible)

jurer: to swear (bad words – insults)

➤ **sans** – **sang** – **cent** mean respectively:

without; blood; one hundred

➤ **si:** if

si: so

si: yes

➤ **terrible:** terrible

C'était un accident terrible: It was a terrible accident.
C'était terrible: It was awful.

terrible: great

Cet homme est terrible: This man is great.
Ce spectacle était terrible: This show was great.

➤ **Jean veut:** Jean wants

J'en veux: I want some

English into French

➤ the will: **la volonté** (will to do something)

the   will: **le   testament**   (last   will)

6

Words starting with an 'h'

Sometimes we link the article with a word starting with an "H", sometimes we don't. For example, we say **les (z)horloges** but not **les (z)héros**.

List of words starting with a 'z' sound (linked) if used in the plural

la hache (n, *f*): the axe

hagard (adj): haggard

la haie (n, *f*): the hedge

le haillon (n, *m*): the rag

la haine (n, *f*): the hatred

haïr (v): to hate

le hall (n, *m*): the corridor

le halo (n, *m*): the halo

la halte (n, *f*): the halt

le hamac (n, *m*): the hammock

le hamburger (n, *m*): the hamburger

le hameau (n, *m*): the hamlet

le hamster (n, *m*): the hamster

la hanche (n, *f*): the hip

le handicap (n, *m*): the handicap, disability

le hangar (n, *m*): the shed, depot, warehouse

hanter (v): to haunt

happer (v): to grab, to seize

harceler (v): to harass, to pester

hardi (adj): bold, self-assured, courageous

le harem (n, *m*): the harem

le hareng (n, *m*): the red herring, the bloater

le harfang (n, *m*): the snowy owl

la hargne (n, *f*): the hostility, belligerence

le haricot (n, *m*): the bean

le harnais (n, *m*): the harness

la harpe (n, *f*): the harp

la hate (n, *f*): the hate

la hausse (n, *f*): the increase

le haut (n, *m*): the top

la haute (n, *f*): the top

le havre (n, *m*): the harbour

le hazard (n, *m*): the chance

hennir (v): to neigh

hérisser (v): to bristle, to make angry

la hernie (n, *f*): the hernia

le héron (n, *m*): the heron

le héros (n, *m*): the hero

le hêtre (n, *m*): the beech

heurter (v): to hit

le hibou (n, *m*): the owl

le hic (n, *m*): the snag

la hideur (n, *f*): the hideousness

la hiérarchie (n, *f*): the hierarchy

le hiéroglyphe (n, *m*): the hieroglyph

le/la hippie (n, *m* or *f*): the hippy

le hocher (n, *m*): the rattle

le hockey (n, *m*): hockey

la Hollande (n, *f*): the Netherlands

le homard (n, *m*): the lobster

la honte (n, *f*): shame

le hoquet (n, *m*): the hiccough

la horde (n, *f*): the horde or pack

hors (prep): excluding

la hotte (n, *f*): the wicker basket or cooker hood

le houblon (n, *m*): the hop

la houle (n, *f*): the swell (sea)

la housse (n, *f*): the slipcover, the pillowcase

le huard (n, *m*): the loonie

le hublot (n, *m*): the porthole

huer (v): to boo

huit: eight

humer (v): to smell

hurler (v): to scream

le huron (n, *m*): Huron

la hutte (n, *f*): the hut

List of words starting with a silent 'h'

habile (adj): clever

l'habit (n, *m*): the habit (clothing)

habiter (v): to live

l'habitude (n, *f*): the habit, the practice

l'haleine (n, *f*): breath

l'hallali (n, *m*): the mort, the kill

halluciner (v): to hallucinate

l'haltère (n, *m*): the dumbbell

l'hameçon (n, *m*): hook (fish)

l'harmonie (n, *f*): harmony

héberger (v): to shelter, to host

l'hécatombe (n, *f*): slaughter, bloodshed

l'hégémonie (n, *f*): hegemony, supremacy

l'hélice (n, *f*): the propeller

l'hélicoptère (n, *m*): the helicopter

l'hélium (n, *m*): helium

l'hérésie (n, *f*): heresy

41

hériter (v): to inherit

l'héritier (n, *m*): the heir

l'héritière (n, *f*): the heiress

hermétique (adj): hermetic

l'hermine (n, *f*): ermine

l'héroïne (n, *f*): the heroin

hier (adv): yesterday

l'hilarité (n, *f*): hilarity

l'hirondelle (n, *f*): the swallow

l'histoire (n, *f*): the history

l'hiver (n, *m*): the winter

l'honneur (n, *m*): honour

l'horreur (n, *f*): the horror

l'huissier (n, *m*): the bailiff

l'huître (n, *f*): the oyster

l'hyène (n, *f*): the hyena

7

French words where you pronounce the last letter, even when it is not linked to a vowel or an 'h'

List of words where you pronounce the last consonant all the time [including all words ending with 'if', e.g. **sportif**, or 'al', e.g. **final**...]

animal (n, *m*): animal

apéritif (n, *m*): aperitif

attentif (n, *m*): attentive

bec (n, *m*): beak

boeuf (n, *m*): beef

chacal (n, *m*): jackal

chenil (n, *m*): kennel

cheval (n, *m*): horse

exact (adj, *m*): exact, true

fait (*m*) in the expression '**de ce fait**' or '**en fait**': in fact

fier (adj, *m*): proud

fils (n, *m*): son

fil (n, *m*): thread

final (adj, *m*): final

four (n, *m*): oven

gent (n, *f*): sex

hier: yesterday

inox (n, *m*): stainless steel

jadis (adv): long ago

journal (n, *m*): newspaper

métis (n, *m*): mixed race, mixed blood, blended

miel (n, *m*): honey

moeurs (n, *m*): customs

neuf (adj, *m*): new

oeuf (n, *m*): egg

public (n, *m*): public, audience

rationnel (adj, *m*): rational

sauf: except

set de table (n, *m*): coaster

tournevis (n, *m*): screwdriver

traditionnel (adj, *m*): traditional

transit (n, *m*): transit, trade

tribunal (n, *m*): tribunal

veuf (n, *m*): widower

viaduc (n, *m*): viaduct

vol (n, *m*): flight or theft

8

Other pronunciation irregularities

List of words where the 't' is pronounced like an 's'

arts martiaux

calvitie

égyptien, égyptienne

impatient(e)

inertie

initié(e)

minutieux, minutieuse, minutie

nutritionnel

patience

patient, patiente (first 't')

potentiel (second 't')

prophétie

proportionné, proportionnée

tertiaire

tortionnaire

vénitien, vénitienn

Words where we don't pronounce the 'p':

comptable (n, *m*): accountant

comptabilité (n, *f*): accountancy

sculpté(e) (adj): sculptered

sculpteur, sculpteuse (n, *m* and *f*): scupltor

sept: seven

septième: seventh

Words where we pronounce the 'th' like a 't':

gothique

hypothèque

hypothèse

néogothique

théorie

9

Unfamiliar French idioms

A

A bon entendeur, salut! Once and for all, goodbye!

à bras le corps: arms round the waist

à brûle-pourpoint: Suddenly, without warning

A chacun ses goûts: Each to their own.

acheter en gros: to buy wholesale

à cloche-pied: to hop

à corps perdu: recklessly

à double tour: to double lock

à fond de train: at full speed, at full tilt

aimer son prochain: to love one's neighbour

A la bonne heure! Good for you!/That's the spirit!/ Well done!

à la fortune du pot: to take potluck

à la queue leu-leu: in single file

à l'article de la mort: at the point of death, at death's door

à la une: on the front page

aller à fond de train: to go flat out

aller à la dérive: to drift

aller au fil de l'eau: to drift

aller/courir ventre à terre: to go/run flat out (coll.)

aller de concert: to go together

aller son petit bonhomme de chemin: to tootle along

à pas de loup: stealthily

l'accent du Midi: the accent from the South of France

à perte de vue: as far as the eye can see

à plusieurs titres: for several reasons

à point: medium (way the meat is cooked)

appeler un chat un chat: to call a spade a spade

appuyer sur le champignon: to accelerate

arriver à bon port: to arrive safely

arriver à la cheville de quelqu'un: to be in the same league

une assiette anglaise: assorted cold roast meats

A tes/vos souhaits! Bless you!

à tire-d'aile: swiftly

à tour de rôle: in turn

à tout bout de champ: at every turn

au bain-marie: a water bath

au nez et à la barbe de quelqu'un: right under someone's nose

au petit bonheur la chance: at random

au pied de la lettre: literally

au pied levé: at a moment's notice

Au plaisir! See you later!

au premier chef: essentially

au quart de tour: immediately

Au secours! Help!

à tour de rôle: in turn

au train où vont les choses: at this rate, at the rate things are going

un avocat marron: a shady lawyer

avoir bon pied bon oeil: to be hale and hearty

avoir d'autres chats à fouetter: to have other fish to fry, to have something more important to do

avoir de la suite dans les idées: to be single-minded

avoir des doigts de fée: to have nimble fingers

avoir des fourmis: to have pins and needles

avoir des lettres: to be a cultivated person

avoir des pellicules: to have dandruff

avoir des sueurs froides: to be in a cold sweat (coll.)

avoir du bon sens: to be sensible

avoir du chien: to be elegant, to be sexy

avoir du pot, du bol: to be lucky

avoir du vague à l'âme: to be unsettled, to be melancholic

avoir du vent dans les voiles: to be tipsy

avoir de la bouteille: to be long in the tooth

avoir la gorge serrée: to have a lump in one's throat

avoir la langue bien pendue: to have a ready tongue

avoir la puce à l'oreille: to suspect

avoir le bras long: to be influential

avoir le coeur sur la main: to be generous

avoir le coup d'oeil: to have a good eye

avoir le gosier sec: to have a dry throat

avoir le mal du pays: to be homesick

avoir le monde à ses pieds: to have the world at one's feet

avoir le pied marin: to be a good sailor

avoir les foies: to be scared stiff

avoir les jambes en coton: to have one's legs turn to jelly

avoir les mains baladeuses: to have wandering hands

avoir les nerfs à fleur de peau: to be on edge

avoir les yeux plus grands que le ventre: to bite off more than one can chew

avoir le trac: to have stage fright

avoir le vent en poupe: to have the wind in one's sails

avoir maille à partir avec quelqu'un: to have a bone to pick with someone

avoir mal au coeur: to feel sick

avoir/prendre le fou rire: to laugh uncontrollably

avoir son franc parler: to not mince one's words

avoir quelqu'un à la bonne: to be fond of somebody

avoir/tenir quelqu'un à l'oeil: to keep an eye on someone

avoir quelqu'un à ses trousses: to have someone on one's tail

l'avoir sur le bout de la langue: to be on the tip of one's tongue

avoir toujours le mot pour rire: to be a born joker, to be always ready for a laugh

avoir un air emprunté: to look uncomfortable

avoir un chat dans la gorge: to have a frog in one's throat

avoir un cheveu sur la langue: to have a lisp

avoir une dent contre quelqu'un: to have something against somebody

avoir une faim de loup: to be famished

avoir un mal de chien: to struggle

avoir une mine de papier mâché: to look washed out, to look like death warmed up (coll.)

avoir une peur bleue de: to be dead scared of

avoir une veine de pendu: to be very lucky

avoir un trou de mémoire: to have a lapse of memory, to have one's mind go blank

avoir un type accentué: to be marked

avoir voix au chapitre: to have a say in the matter

à vol d'oiseau: as the crow flies

à vue de nez: at a rough estimate

B

une baleine de parapluie: an umbrella rib

un ballon d'essai: a trial run

un ballot: a nitwit (coll.)

battre de l'aile: to flounder

battre froid à quelqu'un: to give someone the cold shoulder

battre son plein: to be in full swing

bêcheur (un): a toffee-nosed person

une bête à bon Dieu (saying): a ladybird

une bicoque: a small house of mediocre appearance; a shack

bien se porter: to be well (also: to be plump)

un bifteck bleu: a very rare steak

une boîte de nuit: a nightclub

bon comme la romaine: done for

une bonne (obs.)**:** a maid

un bon poste: a good job

un bouchon: a traffic jam

un boute-en-train: a fun person

bouche en cul de poule: pursed lips

la brebis galeuse: the black sheep

bredouiller une excuse: to mumble an apology

brosser un tableau: to describe

broyer du noir: to be down in the dumps (coll.), to be depressed

le bruit court: rumour has it

brûler la chandelle par les deux bouts: to burn the candle at both ends

brûler les étapes: to rush things

brûler un feu rouge: to go through a red light

C

un cadavre ambulant: death warmed up

Ça me fait froid dans le dos: It sends shivers down my spine.

Ça n'a pas l'air catholique: It looks shady.

un canard: a rag (coll.) (i.e. a newspaper)

ça ne court pas les rues: to be rare

Ça ne mange pas de pain: It is not important.

un casse-pied: a bore, a pain in the neck (coll.)

Cause toujours, tu m'intéresses: You can always talk, but you don't impress me.

ça va, ça vient: on again, off again; easy come, easy go

Ça vaut le coup; cela vaut la peine: It's worth it; it's worth the trouble.

Ça y est! That's it!

Cela crève les yeux: It's staring you in the face; it's as plain as the nose on your face.

Cela me soulève le coeur: It makes me sick (coll.) (subjectively); it turns my stomach (physically).

Cela m'est égal: It makes no difference; it's all the same.

Cela mettra du beurre dans les épinards: That will swell the coffers a little; that will make life a little easier.

Cela n'a rien à voir avec...: It has nothing to do with...

Cela me fait mal au coeur: It disgusts me; it grieves me.

Cela ne me fait ni chaud ni froid: I'm not at all bothered.

Cela saute aux yeux: It's obvious.

Cela va de soi: It goes without saying, it stands to reason.

Ce n'est pas commode: It is not easy.

ce n'est pas demain la veille: to not be about to do something

Ce n'est pas la mer à boire: It's not as bad as all that; it's not that difficult.

Ce n'est pas le mauvais cheval: He is not a bad guy.

C'est à double tranchant: It cuts both ways.

C'est à vous fendre l'âme: It breaks my heart.

C'est bête comme chou: It's child's play; it's as easy as pie.

C'est bidon: It's baloney.

C'est bien fait pour toi: It serves you right.

C'est bien le fils de son père: He's a chip off the old block.

C'est bonnet blanc et blanc bonnet: It's exactly the same; it's one and the same.

C'est de bonne guerre: Fair's fair.

c'est du pareil au même: to be as broad as it is long

C'est du propre! Well done! (ironical)

C'est du tout cuit: It's in the bag.

C'est gros comme une maison: It is as plain as the nose on your face.

C'est la goutte d'eau qui fait déborder le vase: It's the last straw.

C'est le bouquet! That takes the biscuit!

C'est le cadet de mes soucis: It is the least of my problems.

C'est n'importe quoi: That is nonsense.

C'est parti comme en quatorze: It started well.

C'est plus fort que moi: I can't help it.

C'est son chou-chou: He is her favourite.

C'est son rayon: That's his line. (coll.)

C'est super chouette: It is fantastic.

C'est une histoire à dormer debout: It's a cock-and-bull story.

C'est un travail de longue haleine: It's an exacting task.

C'est ma bête noire: That's my pet hate; I can't stand it.

chair de poule: goose flesh

changer son fusil d'épaule: to change sides

Chat échaudé craint l'eau froide: Once bitten, twice shy. (prov.)

un chef-d'oeuvre: a masterpiece, a work of art

chercher la petite bête: to nitpick

chercher midi à quatorze heures: to look for complications

les cheveux en bataille: dishevelled hair

chinoiseries administratives: red tape

cinq colonnes à la une: front page

les clous: the pedestrian crossing

une combine: a scheme

comme ci, comme ça: so-so (coll.)

comme un poisson dans l'eau: in one's element

un complet rayé: a pinstriped suit

compter pour du beurre: to count for nothing

un conseil d'administration: a board of directors

corps et biens: all hands on deck

coucher à la belle étoile: to sleep in the open air at night

un coup de fil: a phone call

un coup de foudre: love at first sight

un coup de pouce: a helping hand

couper la poire en deux: to split the difference

couper les cheveux en quatre: to split hairs

coup sur coup: in close succession

courir les rues: commonplace

courir sur le haricot: to get on someone's nerves

cousu de fil blanc: blatant, too obvious to fool anyone

coûte que coûte: at all costs; come what may; whatever you do

coûter les yeux de la tête: to cost the earth (coll.); to cost a fortune; to be very expensive

coûter un bras: to cost a fortune

crêper le chignon: to fight (among women)

crever les yeux: to be obvious

Croix de bois, croix de fer, si je mens je vais en enfer: Cross my heart and hope to die.

un croque-monsieur: a toasted ham and cheese sandwich

culottes bouffantes: baggy trousers

D

dans la fleur de l'âge: in the prime of one's life

dans la foulée: at the same time

dans le blanc des yeux: straight in the eye

dans le plus simple appareil: in one's birthday suit

dans le vent: with it (coll.)

découvrir le pot aux roses (un secret): to get to the bottom of it

dans tous les coins et recoins: in every nook and cranny

d'arrache-pied: flat out (coll.)

de bon coeur: willingly

de bouche à oreille: by word of mouth

de but en blanc: point blank, just like that (coll.), at the drop of a hat

de fil en aiguille: gradually, little by little, one thing leading to another

de guerre lasse: finally

de longue haleine: long-term

déménager à la cloche de bois: to do a moonlight flit (coll.)

de nos jours: nowadays

de pacotille: cheap (sometimes tacky)

de plein fouet: head-on (accident)

de pied en cap: elegant

de prime abord: at first glance

le dernier cri: the latest fashion

détaler comme un lièvre: to escape very fast

dire à quelqu'un ses quatre vérités: to tell someone a few home truths

un doigt de: a drop of

donner carte blanche à quelqu'un: to give someone a free hand

donner du fil à retordre à quelqu'un: to give someone a hard time

donner/passer un coup de fil à quelqu'un: to give someone a ring

donner sa langue au chat: to give up

donner un coup de main: to lend a hand

dormir à poings fermés: to be sound asleep

dormir sur ses deux oreilles: to sleep soundly

un drôle de zèbre: a peculiar person

dur de la feuille: hard of hearing

E

l'échapper belle: to have a narrow escape

écrire des tartines: to write a lot

un effet boeuf: an impressive effect

Elle est fleur bleue: She is a prude.

emprunter une route: to take a road

en avoir le coeur net: to check

en boucher un coin à quelqu'un: to knock someone sideways

en connaître un rayon: to know a lot

en cuire: to be sorry (i.e. regret something)
Example: **Il va t'en cuire s'ils apprennent que tu as triché.**

endetté jusqu'au cou: up to one's ears in debt (coll.)

en donner sa tête à couper: to bet one's life on it (coll.)

en faire à sa tête: to go one's own way

en faire voir de toutes les couleurs à quelqu'un: to give someone a hard time

en moins de deux; en moins de rien: in a flash; in less than no time

en odeur de sainteté: in somebody's good graces

en prendre son parti: to have to accept something

enregistrer ses bagages: to check in luggage

en somme: all in all

entre chien et loup: in the twilight

entre quatre yeux: between you and me

entrer en ligne de compte: to take into consideration

en un tour de main: in a flash

en veux-tu, en voilà: as many as you want

en voir trente-six chandelles: to see stars

état de siège: siege

étouffer/tuer une idée dans l'oeuf: to nip an idea in the bud

être à même de: to be able to

être à plat: to be washed out

être au garde-à-vous: to be standing to attention

être aux anges: to be on cloud nine (coll.); to be over the moon

être à cheval sur ses principes: to be a stickler for principles

être à court de liquide: to be short of ready cash

être au courant: to be informed, to know about

être à couteaux tirés: to be on bad terms

être au parfum: to be aware of

être au point-mort: to be at a standstill

être aux abois: to be at your last gasp (coll.), to be desperate

être aux cent coups: to be at one's wits' end

être aux prises: to be grappling with

être belle à croquer: to be as pretty as a picture

être cloué au lit: to be bedridden

être beurré: to be pickled

être chocolat: to have been swindled

être comme cul et chemise: to be best friends

être comme le beau jour et la nuit: as different as night and day

être comme un coq en pâte: to be/live in clover

être dans de beaux draps: to be in a fix

être dans la lune: to have one's head in the clouds

être dans les petits/bons papiers de quelqu'un: to be in somebody's good books

être dans son assiette: to feel good

être en berne: to be at half-mast

être en nage: to be covered in sweat (coll.)

être fait comme un rat: to be cornered, to be done for

être fier comme un coq: to be as proud as a peacock

être gros-Jean comme devant: to be back to square one, to be no better off

être la coqueluche d'un groupe: to be the favourite

être la tête de Turc: to be the scapegoat

être logés à la même enseigne: to be in the same boat

être mal en point: to be in a bad state (of health); to be poorly

être mal tourné: to be in a bad mood

être payé pour le savoir: to learn things the hard way

être réservé(e): to be shy

être sans le sou: to be penniless

être sous les drapeaux: to be doing national service

être sur des charbons ardents: to be like a cat on hot bricks (coll.), to be on tenterhooks

être sur la paille: to be desperately poor, to be destitute

être sur le qui-vive: to be on the alert

être tout sucre tout miel: to be all sweetness and light

être très soupe au lait: to fly off the handle easily, to be very quick-tempered

être une fine mouche: to be shrewd

être un homme de plume: to be a writer

être un ours mal léché: to be unpleasant

être un raté: to have failed in life

être vieux jeu: to be old-fashioned

examiner quelquechose sous toutes les coutures: to examine something from every angle

une excuse vaseuse: a lame excuse

F

faire chanter quelqu'un: to blackmail someone

faire chou blanc: to draw a blank; to fail completely

faire courir le bruit: to spread a rumour

faire cul sec: to down in one

faire défaut: to lack

faire des pieds et des mains: to move heaven and earth

faire des ronds de jambes: to bow and scrape

faire d'une pierre deux coups: to kill two birds with one stone

faire du vol à voile: to glide

faire faux bond: to stand someone up

faire grise mine: to look grumpy

faire la courte échelle à quelqu'un: to give someone a leg up

faire la grasse matinée: to have a lie-in

faire la sourde oreille: to turn a deaf ear

faire le beau: to sit up and beg (for dogs)

faire l'école buissonnière: to play truant

faire le pied de grue: to kick one's heels (coll.)

faire le point: to take stock

faire les cent pas: to pace up and down

faire les commissions: to go shopping

faire le siège: to lay siege to

faire les quatre cents coups: to get up to all sorts of tricks (coll.)

faire mal à quelqu'un: to hurt someone

faire marcher à la baguette: to rule someone with a rod of iron

faire mouche: to hit home, to score a goal

faire le jeu de quelqu'un: to play into someone's hands

faire le pont: to make a long weekend of it

faire mouche: to hit the bullseye

faire peau neuve: to turn over a new leaf

faire pencher la balance en faveur de/au detriment de: to tip the scales in favour of/against

faire quelquechose par-dessous la jambe: to do something in a slipshod fashion

faire recette: to take money (at the box office)

faire ses besoins: to 'spend a penny', to go to the toilet

faire signe du doigt/de la main à quelqu'un: to beckon someone

faire sauter une contravention: to use influence to avoid penalty

faire son petit bonhomme de chemin: to do quite nicely (coll.)

faire table rase: to make a clean sweep

faire tâche d'huile/faire boule de neige: to gain ground; to gather momentum; to snowball

faire tapisserie: to be a wallflower (coll.)

faire un bid: to have egg on your face

faire un canard: to hit the wrong note

faire un créneau: to reverse-park a car between two other cars

faire une croix sur quelquechose: to give something up for good

faire une gaffe: to make a blunder

faire une sortie à quelqu'un: to bail somebody out

faire une sale tête: to have an ugly mug (coll.)

faire un four: to flop, to be a fiasco

faire un malheur: to be very successful

faire un pied de nez: to thumb one's nose

faire un prix d'ami à quelqu'un: to knock a bit off for someone (coll.); to let someone have something cheap

faire un renvoi: to belch

faire un saut quelque part: to pop somewhere (coll.)

fausser compagnie à quelqu'un: to give someone the slip

un faux-filet: a type of steak

une fenêtre à guillotine: a sash window

fermer les yeux (sur): to turn a blind eye (to)

un feu de joie: a bonfire

filer à l'anglaise: to take French leave

filer un mauvais coton: to be in a bad way (health)

finir en beauté: to end in glory

finir en queue de poisson: to fizzle out/to end in disappointment

foudroyer quelqu'un du regard: to glare at someone, to look daggers at someone, to give someone a withering look

les frais généraux: the overheads

la franchise postale: freepost

friser la cinquantaire: to be getting on for fifty

des fruits de mer: seafood

G

un gagne-pain: a job that pays the bills

gagner à être connu: to be worth knowing/to grow on someone

gagner les doigts dans le nez: to win hands down

Garde-à-vous! Attention!

garder quelquechose pour la bonne bouche: to keep something up one's sleeve

garder un chien de sa chienne: to have it in for someone

garder une dent contre: to bear a grudge against

garder une poire pour la soif: to save something for a
rainy day

glisser comme une anguille: to be elusive, uncatchable

une grêve du zèle: a work-to-rule campaign

gros Jean comme devant: like a booby (coll.)

un gros mot: a rude word

H

haut de gamme: higher-priced products

haut la main: easily
(e.g. **J'ai réussi mon examen haut la main**)

histoire de rire: just for fun, for a laugh

I

Il est onze heures sonnées: It's gone eleven.

Il était moins cinq/moins une: It was a close shave; it
was a narrow escape.

Il/elle a fait l'X: He/she studied at the Polytechnic Institute.

Il/elle m'a monté un bateau: He/she led me up the garden path.

Il/elle n'a pas inventé le fil à couper le beurre: He/she's not a very bright spark (coll.); he/she will never set the Thames on fire.

Il/elle ne pense qu'à ça: He/she has a dirty mind.

Il/elle n'est pas regardant(e): He/she is not fussy.

Il n'y a pas grand monde: There aren't many people.

Il n'y avait pas un chat: There was not a soul.

Il/elle n'y en a eu que pour quelqu'un: He/she stole the show.

Il/elle tombe à point nommé: He/she comes just in time.

Il y a du monde au balcon: She is big-busted.

Il y a une ombre au tableau: There's a fly in the ointment.

J

J'ai tout lieu de croire…: Everything leads me to believe…

Je n'ai pas la pêche: I am a bit down.

J'étais à mille lieues de penser que: I would never have dreamt that...; it would never have entered my mind that...

Je t'aime bien: I like you.
    Compare:
    ➤ **Je t'aime:** I love you. (Less is more.)
    It also applies for:
    ➤ **J'aime bien ce film mais j'aime celui-là.**

J'ai toujours mal aux cheveux le dimanche: I always have hangovers on Sundays!

Je me sens toute chose: I feel under the weather.

Je me suis fait incendier: I was told off.

J'en passe et des meilleures! And that's not all.

jeter l'éponge: to give up, to throw in the towel

jeter un pavé dans la mare: to set the cat among the pigeons

Je m'en bats l'oeil: I don't give a hoot.

Je n'en mettrais pas la main au feu: I couldn't swear to it.

Je vais vous montrer un peu de quell bois je me chauffe: I'll show you what I am made of.

joindre les deux bouts: to make ends meet

jouer de malheur: to have a run of bad luck, to be dogged by bad luck (coll.)

jouer le tout pour le tout: to risk everything

jouer son va-tout: to play one's last card

jouer sur les deux tableaux: to lay odds both ways

jusqu'au bout des ongles: through and through

J'y suis: I get you (coll.), I'm with you.

L

La balle est dans son camp: The ball is in his court.

La bourse ou la vie! Your money or your life!

laisser tomber: to forget about it

laisser tomber quelqu'un: to jilt someone

une langue de chat: a finger biscuit

langue vivante: spoken language

Le cachet de la poste faisant foi: Date as post mark.

Le champ est libre: The coast is clear.

Le jeu n'en vaut pas la chandelle: It is not worth it.

Le monde appartient à ceux qui se lèvent tôt: The early bird catches the worm. (prov.)

le qu'en dira-t-on: what the neighbours may say

Les absents ont toujours tort: Those who are absent are always in the wrong.

Les fonds sont bas: Funds are low.

Les murs ont des oreilles: Walls have ears.

Le tour est joué: The trick has worked.

lever le pied: to slow down (mainly whilst driving)

L'herbe est toujours plus verte chez le voisin: The grass is always greener on the other side. (prov.)

loin des yeux, loin du coeur: out of sight, out of mind

M

la main dans le sac: red-handed

maison de passe: disorderly house

mal se porter: to be unwell

un mandat d'amener: writ of arrest

manger de la vache enragée: to find it hard to make ends meet

un mauvais pas: a tight corner

ménager la chèvre et le chou: to sit on the fence

mener quelqu'un par le bout du nez: to have someone under one's thumb

le menu fretin: small fry

mettre à pied: to dismiss

mettre à sac: to rifle

mettre dans le mille/être en plein dans le mille: to be bang on target (coll.); to be spot on (coll.)

mettre de l'eau dans son vin: to mellow

mettre des bâtons dans les roues: to put a spoke in someone's wheel; to throw a spanner in the works

mettre en demeure: to oblige

mettre en marche: to start up

mettre en quarantaine: to send to Coventry (coll.)

mettre la charrue devant les boeufs: to put the cart before the horse

mettre la puce à l'oreille de quelqu'un: to arouse someone's suspicion

mettre le doigt dans l'engrenage: to become involved in something

mettre le paquet: to pull out all the stops

mettre les bouchées doubles: to work very hard, to work at twice the speed

mettre les pieds dans le plat: to put one's foot in it (coll.)

mettre sur pied: to set up

mettre tous ses oeufs dans le même panier: to put all one's eggs into one basket (coll.)

le Midi: South of France
i.e: **Je vais aller en vacances dans le Midi**.

Mieux vaut prévenir que guérir (prov.)**:** Prevention is better than cure. (prov.)

mi-figue, mi-raisin: neither fish nor fowl; half-hearted

une mise en train: a warm-up

Mon sang n'a fait qu'un tour: My heart skipped a beat.

monter en épingle: to make a mountain out of a molehill

monter en flèche: to soar/to shoot up (for prices)

monter sur les planches: to go on the stage

Motus et bouche cousue! Keep it under your hat! (coll.), Mum's the word! (coll.)

mourir à petit feu: to fade away

mourir de faim: to be starving

un mouton de panurge: a sheep (coll.), someone who follows others without any thought

myope comme une taupe: as blind as a bat

N

nature morte: still life

n'avoir ni queue ni tête: to make no sense

n'écouter que d'une oreille: to half listen

ne dormer que d'un oeil: to sleep with one eye open, to catnap

ne faire ni une ni deux: to decide straight away

ne pas avoir froid aux yeux: to be plucky

ne pas chômer: to be very busy working

ne pas dire un traître mot: to not say a single word

ne pas en croire ses yeux: to not believe your eyes

ne pas en perdre le sommeil pour autant: to not lose any sleep over it

ne pas en revenir: to be unable to get over something (through surprise)

ne pas en savoir lourd: to not know much about

ne pas être dans son assiette: to be a bit off colour (coll.), to be out of sorts (coll.)

ne pas être tombé de la dernière pluie: to have not been born yesterday

ne pas être très brilliant: to not be too good (health)

ne pas fermer l'oeil: to not sleep a wink

Ne pas jeter le manche après la cognée: Don't put the cart before the horse.

ne pas mâcher ses mots: to not mince one's words

ne pas pouvoir voir quelqu'un en peinture: to hate somebody

ne pas prendre quelquechose pour argent comptant: to take something with a pinch of salt

ne pas réveiller le chat qui dort (prov.): to let sleeping dogs lie (prov.)

ne pas savoir à quel saint se vouer: to not know which way to turn

ne pas savoir où donner de la tête: to not know where to start

ne pas y aller par quatre chemins: to not beat about the bush; to come straight to the point

ne plus se tenir sur ses jambes: to be hardly able to stand

ne tenir qu'à un fil: to hang by a thread

un nid de poule: a pothole (in the road)

un noeud-papillon: a bow tie

un nom à coucher dehors: an impossible name

Nous ne sommes pas sortis de l'auberge: We are not out of the wood.

n'y voir que du bleu: to not smell a rat

O

oeil de boeuf: a round dormer window

On aurait entendu voler une mouche: You could have heard a pin drop.

On devra me passer sur le corps! Over my dead body!

On n'y a vu que du feu: You hardly had time to blink.

Où as-tu la tête? Whatever are you thinking of?

Oui, quand les poules auront des dents! Yes, and pigs might fly!

Oui, quand les poules porteront les oeufs au marché! Yes, and pigs might fly!

P

par-dessus le marché: into the bargain, on top of that

parler à bâtons rompus: to talk about this and that, to speak a lot

par les temps qui courent: the way things are at the moment

par mégarde: by mistake

pas mal: not bad

pas mal de gens: quite a few people

passer à la casserole: to be killed or to get laid

passer au fil de l'épée: to run someone through with a sword

passer du coq à l'âne: to change the subject willy-nilly

passer inaperçu: to go unnoticed

passer la main dans le dos: to flatter

passer l'arme à gauche: to kick the bucket (coll.)

passer l'éponge: to wipe the slate clean (coll.), to forget it

passer son bac: to graduate

passer sur le billiard: to have an operation

payer les pots cassés: to carry the can (coll.), to pay for the damage

passer une nuit blanche: to spend a sleepless night

une peau de chagrin: shagreen leather

pédaler dans la choucroute: to be mixed up

perdre le fil: to lose the thread

personne ne lui arrive à la cheville: no-one can compare; they're head and shoulders above the rest

mon petit chou: my little darling

mon petit doigt me l'a dit: a little bird told me

une petite main: a dressmaker's apprentice

une planche de salut: a lifeline

une poule mouillée: a chicken (coll.), a wimp

un petit four: a small cake

une pomme de discorde: a bone of contention

un pense-bête: a reminder

un petit-suisse: a soft cream cheese

un peu juste: rather a tight fit

pièce rapportée: relation by marriage

pied-de-poule: houndstooth pattern

piquer au vif: to cut to the quick

Plus on est de fous, plus on rit! The more the merrier!

poisson d'avril: April fool

pommes de terre en robe de chambre/pommes de terre en robe des champs: jacket potatoes

un pont en dos d'âne: a humpbacked bridge

un pot-au-feu: hotpot/stew

un pot-de-vin: a bribe, backhander (coll.)

Pouce! Pax!

pour comble de malheur: to crown it all; on top of all that

Pour un coup d'essai, c'est un coup de maître: It is a very good first attempt.

pour une bouchée de pain/pour trois fois rien: for next to nothing/for a song/for peanuts (coll.)

la première manche: the first round/set

prendre au pied de la lettre: to take literally

prendre la clé des champs: to run off, to head for the hills (coll.)

prendre la mouche: to get huffy

prendre le mors aux dents: to take the bit between one's teeth

prendre quelquechose pour argent comptant: to take something for granted

prendre quelqu'un de court: to take someone aback

prendre quelqu'un en grippe: to take a sudden dislike to someone

prendre quelqu'un sous son aile: to protect someone

prendre ses jambes à son cou: to take to one's heels

prendre une raclée: to take a beating

une prise de bec: an argument

un prix de revient: cost price

Q

Quand le bâtiment va, tout va! *French idiom that means that the economy is going well*

Quel numéro! What a character!

Quelle mouche t'a piqué? What's come over you?

R

la radio: the X-ray

raser les murs: to keep a low profile

rater un gâteau: to badly execute a cake

recommencer à zéro: to start from scratch

un régime de bananes: a bunch of bananas

réglé comme du papier à musique: as regular as clockwork

un règlement de comptes: a settling of scores, a reckoning

rejoindre son corps d'origine/son poste: to rejoin one's regiment

un remède de cheval: a drastic remedy

remuer ciel et terre: to leave no stone unturned

reprendre le dessus: to get over (an illness), to recover

rester bouche bée: to be open-mouthed, to gawp

revenir à soi: to come around

revenir bredouille: to come back empty-handed

Revenons à nos moutons: Let's get back to our topic.

un rhume carabiné: a bad cold

rire à gorge déployée: to roar with laughter

rire dans sa barbe: to laugh into one's sleeve

rire jaune: to give a sickly smile; to give a forced smile

ronger son frein: to champ at the bit

ruer dans les brancards: to become rebellious

S

sabler le champagne: to drink champagne

un sac de noeuds: a can of worms; a problem

sage comme une image: as good as gold

Sa mémoire est une vraie passoire: He has a memory like a sieve. (coll.)

sans crier gare: without warning

sans encombre: without any problem

sans tambour ni trompette: without any fuss

Sauve qui peut! Every man for himself!; Run for your life!

sauver la mise: to get back one's outlay

savoir à quoi s'en tenir: to know where one stands

se casser la tête: to rack one's brains

se creuser la tête: to rack one's brains

se croire sorti de la cuisse dc Jupiter: to think a lot of oneself

se faire du mauvais sang: to be in a real state (coll.)

se faire porter malade: to report sick

se faire tirer l'oreille: to need/take a lot of persuading

se lever du pied gauche: to get out of bed on the wrong side (coll.)

la semaine des quatre jeudis: [never in] a month of Sundays

se méfier de quelquechose comme de la peste: to be highly suspicious of something (like the plague)

se mettre au garde-à-vous: to stand to attention

se mettre en quatre: to bend over backwards (coll.), to go out of one's way

se mettre sur son trente-et-un: to dress up to the nines

se mordre les doigts de quelquechose: to regret something bitterly

s'en donner à coeur joie: to have a great time (coll.)

s'en faire: to worry

s'en faire des montagnes: to make a mountain out of a molehill

s'entendre comme larrons en foire: to be as thick as thieves

sens dessus dessous: to turn upside down

se regarder en chiens de faïence: to look daggers at each other, to glare at each other

se répandre comme une trainée de poudre: to spread like wildfire

serrer les dents: to keep a stiff upper lip

se sentir mal dans sa peau: to feel ill at ease

se sentir mal en train: to feel out of sorts, to not feel good

se sentir toute chose: to feel quite peculiar

se serrer: to squeeze up

se tenir à carreau: to behave well

se tenir les côtes de rire: to split one's sides with laughter

se tuer à la tâche: to kill oneself working

se vendre comme des petits pains: to sell like hot cakes

si cela ne vous fait rien: if you don't mind

si cela te dit: if you fancy it; if you like

siège social: registered office

simple comme bonjour: a piece of cake

soldés: on sale

somme toute: when all is said and done; in the end

son compte est bon: he has had it

soulever un lièvre: to stir up a hornet's nest

sous peu: before long; shortly

sur les bords: a bit – e.g. **Tu exagères sur les bords.**

sur les chapeaux de roue: very fast

T

un temps de chien: bad weather

tenez-moi au courant: keep me informed

tenir quelquechose de bonne source: to have something on good authority

tenir l'affiche: to have a long run

tenir le crachoir à quelqu'un: to hold the floor

tenir le haut du pavé: to lord it

tenir les délais: doing a job and respecting the time limits

tenir sa langue: to hold your tongue

tête à queue: to deliberately swerve in front of another driver

tête-bêche: top to bottom

tiré à quatre épingles: dressed to the nines

tiré par les cheveux: far-fetched

tirer à la courte paille: to draw lots

tirer au flanc: to swing the lead (coll.); to goof off

tirer son chapeau à quelqu'un: to take one's hat off to someone

tirer sur la chasse: to flush (down the toilet)

tomber à plat: to fall flat

tomber comme un cheveu sur la soupe: to come at the worst possible moment

tomber dans le panneau: to fall for it (coll.); to walk right into it (coll.)

tomber en désuétude: to fall into disuse

tomber les quatre fers en l'air: to go sprawling

tomber pile: to happen at the right moment

tomber sur un bec/sur un os: to come up against a snag, to hit a problem

touche-à-tout: to have a finger in every pie

toucher un mot: to mention

toujours est-il que: the fact remains

un tour de rein: a sudden back pain

tourner autour du pot: to beat around the bush

tourner au vinaigre: to turn sour

tous les trente-six du mois: once in a blue moon (coll.)

tout baigne dans l'huile: everything is fine

Toutes les bonnes choses ont une fin: All good things come to an end.

le Tout-Paris: the smart set; the trendy Parisians

tout un chacun: every Tom, Dick and Harry

le train-train: the humdrum routine

traduire quelqu'un en justice: to prosecute

travailler au noir: to moonlight

travailler d'arrache-pied: to work like a navvy

99

trempé jusqu'aux os: soaked to the skin

trouver à qui parler: to meet one's match

Tu parles Charles! You don't say!

U

Une drôle de tête! You should have seen your face!

Un tien vaut mieux que deux tu l'auras. (prov.): A bird in the hand is worth two in the bush. (prov.)

V

vendre la mèche: to let the cat out of the bag; to give the game away

vendre la peau de l'ours avant de l'avoir tué (prov.): to count one's chickens before they have hatched (prov.)

une vie de baton de chaise: a rollicking life

un vieux de la vieille: a very old person

un violon d'Ingres: a hobby

voir la vie en rose: to see everything through rose-tinted glasses

W

un wagon-lit: a sleeping car

Y

y mettre du sien: to pull one's weight

y perdre son latin: to be able to make neither head nor tail of something

10

Typical French idioms, often familiar and used every day

A

à gogo: in abundance, galore, to burn (coll.)

à la gomme: rubbish

à la mords-moi le noeud: dodgy

à la va-comme-je-te-pousse: any which way

aller à toute pompe: to go very fast

aller faire la bombe: to paint the town red

aller au petit coin: to go to the loo

appuyer sur le champignon: to step on the gas, to accelerate

aux frais de la princesse: at Her Majesty's expense

les avoir à zéro: to be frightened

avoir de la brioche/bidon: to have a potbelly

avoir du bagout: to have a gift of the gab (coll.)

avoir du bol/avoir du pot: to be in luck, to be lucky

avoir du chien: to have sex appeal

avoir du pain sur la planche: to have a lot on one's plate

avoir du toupet: to have a cheek

avoir la flemme: to be lazy

avoir la frite: to be feeling great

avoir la gueule de bois: to have a hangover

avoir la tête comme un tambour: to suffer from a headache

avoir le cafard: to have the blues, to be down (coll.)

avoir les idées claires: to have a clear head; to think straight

avoir les foies: to be scared stiff

avoir mal aux cheveux: to have a hangover

avoir quarante ans bien sonnées: to be on the wrong side of forty

avoir quelqu'un dans le nez: to have someone get up one's nose (coll.), to be unable to stand someone

avoir un coup de pompe: to feel tired

avoir une araignée au plafond: to have a screw loose (coll.)

avoir un pépin: to have a problem

avoir un poil dans la main: to be lazy

avoir un verre dans le nez: to have one too many (coll.)

à vue de nez: at a rough guess

B

balancer une vanne: to make a dig (at someone)

battre à plate couture: to beat someone hollow

bavard comme une pie: a chatterbox

bête comme une oie: someone extremely stupid

bigrement: extremely

boire comme un trou: to drink like a fish (coll.)

boire la tasse: to swallow a mouthful (when swimming)

bordélique: messy

bouffer (manger) (fam.): to eat

branché: switched on (coll.)

C

Ça baigne dans l'huile: Everything is going smoothly.

cablé: trendy (coll.)

Ça coûte la peau du cul: It's very expensive.

Ça fait râler: It makes you fume. (coll.)

Ça me fait une belle jambe! A lot of good it does me! (coll.); it won't get me very far.

Ça ne casse pas des briques: It's nothing to write home about.

casser la croûte: to have a snack

casser sa pipe: to kick the bucket (coll.)

Casse-toi! (a bit rude): Go away!

Cela me met en boule: It gets my goat; it makes me mad.

Ce n'est pas de la tarte! It is not easy!

C'est bête: It's silly/it's a pity.

c'est bibi: Muggins here (coll.)

C'est dans la poche! It's in the bag! (coll.)

C'est du pipi de chat: It's as dull as dishwater.

C'est kif-kif: It's the same.

C'est la barbe: It's boring.

C'est la fin des haricots: That's the last straw! (coll.)

C'est une autre paire de manches: It's a different kettle of fish; it's another story.

C'est vachement chouette/bien: It is very nice.

chanter (qu'est-ce que tu me chantes-là?): to tell

chiche que: bet you (coll.)

chiper: to pinch (coll.)

clouer le bec: to shut someone up

coller: to keep someone in (school detention)

coincer la bulle: to do nothing; to laze around

compter pour du beurre: to count for nothing

connaitre quelquechose sur le bout des doigts: to know something by heart

copains comme cochons: inseparable friends

courir sur le haricot: to get on someone's nerves

D

débrouillard: nifty (coll.), streetwise

démerdard(e): a person who knows how to resolve problems

des comptes d'apothicaire: complicated calculations

des larmes de crocodile: crocodile tears (coll.); false tears

du coup: as a result

dur de la feuille: hard of hearing

E

écrire des tartines: to write a lot

en avoir ras le bol: to be fed up with something/to be sick of something (coll.)

en avoir plein le dos: to be fed up with something

en avoir vu des vertes et des pas mûres: to have been through a lot (coll.)

en baver des ronds de chapeau: to have one's tongue hanging out

en cas de pépin: if something goes wrong

en cinq sec: in the twinkling of an eye

en faire tout un plat: to make a fuss (coll.); to make a song and dance (coll.)

en mettre plein la vue: to dazzle someone

en prendre plein son grade: to get a severe telling-off

entendre une mouche voler: to hear a pin drop

En voiture Simone! Go ahead!

envoyer promener: to send packing (coll.)

Et ta soeur? Mind your own business!

être à poil: to be naked

être barbant: to be boring

être bête comme ses pieds: to be as daft as a brush, to be stupid for words

être bien balancée: to be well built

être dans le pétrin: to be in a jam (coll.), to be in a mess (coll.)

être de mauvais poil: to be in a bad mood

être de bon poil: to be in a good mood

être dur à cuire: to put up a strong resistance

être en dehors de ses pompes: to be absent minded

être mal fagoté(e): to be badly dressed

être marteau: to be crazy

être plein(e) aux as: to be filthy rich

être rasoir: to be a bore (coll.)

être sonné: to be knocked out

être timbré: to be round the bend (coll.)

être une poule mouillée: to not be brave; to be a chicken (coll.)

être vaseux: to be washed out

être verni: to be lucky

F

faire des gorges chaudes: to keep people talking; to keep tongues wagging

faire des yeux de merlan frit: to have an inexpressive stare

faire du lèche-vitrine: to go window shopping

faire du plat à quelqu'un: to chat someone up

faire la bringue: to paint the town red

faire la pluie et le beau temps: to run the show

faire le Jacques: to act the fool

faire le poireau: to wait for someone, to be left kicking one's heels (coll.)

faire marcher quelqu'un: to pull someone's leg

faire prendre à quelqu'un des vessies pour des lanternes: to pull the wool over someone's eyes

faire quelquechose à la six quatre deux: to do something in a slapdash way (coll.); to do something any old how (coll.).

faire quelquechose comme un pied: to not have a clue (about how to do something) (coll.)

faire tout un fromage de rien du tout: to be excessively dramatic

faire tout un foin: to make a great song and dance (coll.)

faire une fleur à quelqu'un: to do someone a favour

faire une grosse boulette: to screw the pooch (coll.); to make a big mistake

faire une vacherie à quelqu'un: to play a nasty trick on someone

faire un pied de nez à quelqu'un: to cock a snook at someone

faire un tour de cochon: to trick

flanquer: to deck; to slap

fauché comme les blés: broke (coll.)

une fièvre de cheval: a raging fever

mon frangin/ma frangine: my brother/my sister

un froid de canard: brass monkey weather (coll.); freezing cold weather

G

les gambettes (fam.) *f.*: legs

la grasse matinée: a lie-in

un gros légume: a VIP

I

Il/elle a cinquante balais: He/she is fifty.

Il/elle en tient une couche: He/she is a cretin.

Il/elle est bête: He/she is stupid.

Il/elle est vachement gonflé[e]: He/she has a cheek.

Il/elle va gagner les doigts dans le nez: He/she is going to win hands down.

Il/elle m'a coupé le sifflet: He/she interrupted me.

Il/elle n'a pas un rond: He/she's broke; he/she's skint. (coll.)

Il/elle n'en manque jamais une: He/she blunders/boobs every time; he/she always puts his/her foot in it. (coll.)

Il n'y avait que trois pelés et un tondu: There was hardly anybody there.

Il pleut des cordes: It's bucketing down; it's raining cats and dogs. (coll.)

J

Je m'en contrebalance: I don't give a damn. (coll.)

Je m'en fiche pas mal: I don't give a damn.

J'en ai marre: I've had enough.

jeter l'argent par la fenêtre: to waste money

L

La barbe! What a bore!

La note est plutôt salée: That's pretty steep. (coll.)
  (price)

Les carottes sont cuites! We are done for! (coll.), We've
had it! (coll.)

louper quelquechose: to miss something, or to do it
badly

M

machin/machine: what's-his-name/what's-her-name

une machine à sous: a one-armed bandit (coll.)

manger le morceau: to spill the beans (coll.)

manger sur le pouce: to grab a bite (coll.); to have a
  quick snack

marcher comme sur des roulettes: to go like
  clockwork; to go without a hitch (coll.)

un m'as-tu vu: a conceited person

une Marie-couche-toi-là: a tart

un mec: a guy

un mégot: a dog-end, a cigarette butt

mener une vie de bâton de chaise: to lead the high life

mettre du beurre dans les épinards: to make oneself richer

mettre les bouts: to leave, to split

mettre quelqu'un à l'ombre: to put someone behind bars (coll.)

un moins que rien: a useless person

un/une môme: a kid (boy or girl)

un monde fou: a huge crowd

Mon oeil! My foot! (coll.)

N

ne pas en mener large: to be scared

ne pas être piqué des vers: to be first rate

ne pas faire dans la dentelle: to do something "without frills", without refinement

ne pas pouvoir sentir quelqu'un/ne pas pouvoir voir quelqu'un: to be unable to stand someone

Nom d'une pipe! My god!; Damn!

O

Occupe-toi de tes oignons! Mind your own business!

un oeil au beurre noir: a black eye

On vous casse les bonbons? Are we annoying you?

On vous met des peaux de bananes: Someone is trying to put a spoke in your wheel (create problems for you).

P

les paluches (fam.) *f.*: big hands

parler français comme une vache espagnole: to not speak very good French (coll.)

pas folle la guêpe: not born yesterday

pas franc du collier: fishy

pas piqué des hannetons: great, a helluva...

passer à tabac: to be beaten up; to beat to a pulp

passer un savon à quelqu'un: to shout at, to give someone a rocket (coll.)

perdre la boule: to go off one's rocker (coll.), to go around the twist (coll.), to go crazy

perdre le nord: to go to pieces

le petit coin: the loo (coll.)

piger: to understand

piquer du nez: to drop off to sleep

piquer une crise: to go through the roof (coll.)

piquer une tête: to dive

plier baggage: to leave

le pognon: the money

pomper l'air à quelqu'un: to annoy someone

pompette *f*: tipsy

un portrait tout craché: the spitting image

poser un lapin: to stand someone up

poule de luxe: a high-class call girl

une poule mouillée: a coward, a wimp, a chicken (coll.)

Pour moi, c'est de l'hébreu: It's double Dutch; it's all Greek to me. (coll.)

prendre des vessies pour des lanternes: to think that the moon is made of green cheese (coll.); to make a silk purse out of a sow's ear (coll.)

prendre ses clics et ses clacs: to clean up and clear out

prendre ses jambes à son coup: to leave very quickly

prendre une bûche: to fall

prendre une pelle: to fall flat on one's face

prendre une veste: to come a cropper (coll.)

un propre à rien: a good-for-nothing

Q

Quand les poules auront des dents: It will never happen.

Quelle salade! What a pack of lies!

R

raconter des vertes et des pas mûres: to tell (someone) things that are hard to digest

ramasser une veste: to fail

ramener sa fraise: to show up

reprendre du poil de la bête: to be one's own self again

rester le bec dans l'eau: to be left high and dry

rien à cirer: to not give a damn

Rien à secouer: It's not my problem.

rond comme une queue de pelle: very drunk

S

saler: to be tough on (coll.)

sauver les meubles: to save face

sécher les cours: to play truant

s'en soucier comme de l'an quarante: to not give two hoots (coll.)

se faire de la bile au sujet de: to get worried about

se faire la valise: to leave

se faire sonner les cloches par quelqu'un: to get a good telling off from someone

se ficher de quelqu'un/quelquechose: to not give two hoots for someone/something

se la couler douce: to take it easy

se magner le train: to hurry up

se mettre à table: to talk, to spill the beans

se mettre le doigt dans l'oeil: to have another think coming

se mouiller: to stick one's neck out (coll.)

s'en mettre plein la lampe: to stuff one's face

s'en moquer comme de sa première chemise: to not care two hoots (coll.)

s'en taper: to not care

se payer la tête de quelqu'un: to make fun of someone

se planter: to fail

se regarder le nombril: to see oneself as the center of the universe

serrer la vis à quelqu'un: to crack down hard on someone (coll.)

se serrer les coudes: to back one another up, to stick together (coll.)

se taper la cloche: to eat well

se tâter le pouls: to weigh it up

sucrer les fraises: to be old and doddery

T

un temps de chien: foul/filthy weather (coll.)

tendre l'oreille: to listen attentively

tirer la couverture à soi: to take all the credit; to gain unfair recognition

tirer les vers du nez à quelqu'un: to worm something out of someone (coll.)

tirer au cul: to swing the lead; to shirk one's duty

tomber dans les bras de Morphée: to fall asleep

tomber dans les pommes: to faint; to pass out (coll.)

tomber sur un os: to hit a snag

tordu(e): weird

toujours retomber sur ses pattes: always landing on one's feet (coll.); always getting out of difficult situations

travailler du chapeau: to be crazy

trimer: to work hard

un trou: a dump (coll.)

Tu me pèles le jonc! You get up my nose! (coll.)

Tu peux toujours courir! You can take a running jump!; You can whistle for it!

U

utiliser le système D (démerde): to be very resourceful (to be able to get out of the 'shit')

V

un va-nu-pieds: a very poor person

Va te faire cuire un oeuf! Go away!

Va voir ailleurs si j'y suis! Go away!

un vieux clou: an old banger (coll.)

les vieux: the parents

vieux frère: chum (coll.), pal (coll.)

Vire de là! Go away!

vite fait sur le gaz: very fast

vivre aux crochets de quelqu'un: to sponge off somebody

voir midi à sa porte: to mind one's own business

11

Pronunciation of numbers

Pronounce the ending	Don't pronounce the ending
cinq six sept huit neuf dix	un deux trois quatre

> <u>However</u>: You should pronounce the last letter of all numbers when followed by a word beginning with a vowel or an 'h'.

   i.e. **un an, deux ans, un hôtel**...

> <u>Nevertheless</u>: When a number is followed by a consonant, you don't sound the last letter, even in the numbers **cinq**, **six**, **huit** and **dix**.

   i.e. **cinq minutes** is pronounced *san minutes*.

The same thing applies for any variation these numbers: 25, 36, 48, 110, 1358...

12

Tongue twisters: *virelangues*

These can't be easily translated, but you can email me and I will help you as much as possible if you are interested.

Ah ! pourquoi Pépita sans répis m'épies-tu, dans le puits Pépita pourquoi te tapis-tu ? Tu m'épies sans pitié, c'est piteux de m'épier, de m'épier Pépita ne peux-tu te passer ?

Bonjour Madame la saucissière, combien vendez-vous ces six saucisses-là ?

Un chasseur chassant chasser doit savoir chasser sans son chien.

Ton thé t'a-t-il ôté ta toux ?

Rat vit rôt. Rôt tenta rat. Rat mit patte à rôt. Rôt brûla patte à rat. Rat s'coua patte et quitta rôt.

Tes laitues naissent-elles ? — Yes mes laitues naissent.

La pie niche haut, l'oie niche bas, où l'hibou niche-t-il ?

Qu'a bu l'âne au lac ? — L'âne au lac a bu l'eau.

Le blé s'moud-y, l'habit s'coud-y — Oui, le blé s'moud, l'habit s'coud.

Vos guêtres sèchent-elles ? Ya mes guêtres sèchent.

Les chaussettes de l'archiduchesse sont-elles sèches, archisèches ?

Il était une fois, une marchande de foie qui s'est dit ma foi c'est la première fois et la dernière fois que je vends du foie dans la ville de Foix, il fait trop froid dans la ville de Foix.

Ce chasseur sait chasser sans son chien dit le sage garde-chasse, chasseur sachez chasser sans chien !

Ces Basques se passent ce casque et ce masque jusqu'à ce que ce masque et ce casque se cassent.

Ces cerises sont si sûres qu'on ne sait pas si c'en sont.

C'est l'évadé du Nevada qui dévalait dans la vallée, dans la vallée du Nevada, qu'il dévalait pour s'évader, sur un vilain vélo volé, qu'il a volé dans une villa, et le valet qui fut volé vit l'évadé du Nevada qui dévalait dans la vallée, dans la vallée du Nevada, qu'il dévalait pour s'évader sur un vilain vélo volé.

C'est pas beau mais tentant de tenter de tâter, de téter les tétons de tata quand tonton n'est pas là.

C'est trop tard pour le tram trente-trois.

Tu t'entêtes à tout tenter, tu t'uses et tu te tues à tant t'entêter.

Un pâtissier qui pâtissait chez un tapissier qui tapissait, demanda un jour au tapissier qui tapissait : vaut-il mieux pâtisser chez un tapissier qui tapisse ou tapisser chez un pâtissier qui pâtisse ?

As-tu été à Tahiti ?

Un généreux déjeuner régénérerait des généraux dégénérés.

13

Table of all possessive adjectives

E*: English   F*: French

E*	F*	E*	French		
			Singular		Plural
			Masculine	Feminine	
I	je/j'	my	mon	ma	mes
you	tu	your	ton	ta	tes
he/she	il/elle	his/her	son	sa	ses
		its	son	sa	ses
we	nous	our	notre		nos
you (plural)	nous	your	votre		vos
they	ils/elles	their	leur		leurs

The possessive adjectives agree with the gender of the word that comes next, not the owner.

➤ **c'est mon chien**

  c'est ma maison

  ce sont mes parents

➤ **c'est ton livre**

  c'est ta sœur

  ce sont tes cahiers

➤ **son ballon**

  sa mère

  ses photos

➤ **notre voiture**

  nos vélos

➤ **votre jardin**

  vos tickets

> **leur argent**

> **leurs animaux**

Exception – feminine words starting with a vowel or an 'h':

> **mon ami**

> **mon amie**

> **ton ami**

> **ton amie**

> **son ami**

> **son amie**

14

Expressions that are useful when you are driving in France

Firstly, there is a motorist advice centre giving useful traffic information on the radio; it is called **Bison Fûté**.

chaussée rétrécie/rétrécissement: narrowing road

dos d'âne: sleeping policemen, speed bumps

embouteillages: traffic jams

feux: traffic lights

passage à niveau: train gate, level crossing

permis de conduire: driving licence

ralentir: slow down

roulez à droite: drive on the right

route verte: quiet road

verglas: black ice

15

Expressions that you should not translate literally

- > *I am hot:* Don't translate literally! **Je suis chaud(e)** means "I am horny".

- > *I am cold:* **je suis froid(e)** means "I am frigid".

- > *I am on the train:* **je suis <u>dans</u> le train**

- > *I feel:* **je ressens**

  I resent: **je n'aime pas**

- > *I introduce myself:* Don't say **je m'introduis** (means "I go in") but **je me présente**.

- > *I attend:* Don't say **j'attends** (means "I wait") but **j'assiste à**.

> ➢ *the mind map:* Don't say **la carte mentale** (just wrong) but **l'organigramme.**

> ➢ *rude:* **impoli(e)**

> ➢ *hard:* **dur(e)**

16

Tips for success

Climbing the language mountain

Plan your journey in stages.

Set goals.

The journey is hardest at the start.

It starts to get much easier after A2.

Expect some fog early on. Stick it out.

This is one mountain you can't fall off!

You'll reach a point of sudden clarification.

Do anything to get more exposure.

Be resourceful – there's more than one route up!

Get tested frequently to find out where you are or if you're making mistakes without realising it.

Go back if you need to! Be organised.

Learn about learning to go faster if needed.

My gift to all you literary folks

L'accent
un poème de Miguel Zamacoïs

Before I finish this book, I want to share with you one of
the best poems ever written about accents.

De l'accent ? De l'accent ? Mais, après tout, en ai-je ?
Pourquoi cette faveur ? Pourquoi ce privilège ?
Et si je vous disais à mon tour, gens du Nord
Que c'est vous qui, pour nous, semblez l'avoir très fort
Que nous disons de vous, du Rhône à la Gironde
"Ces gens-là n'ont pas le parler de tout le monde"
Et que, tout dépendant de la façon de voir,
Ne pas avoir d'accent, pour nous, c'est en avoir

Eh bien non, je blasphème et je suis las de feindre
Ceux qui n'ont pas d'accent, je ne peux que les plaindre

Emporter avec soi son accent familier
C'est emporter un peu sa terre à ses souliers
Emporter son accent d'Auvergne ou de Bretagne
C'est emporter un peu sa lande ou sa montagne
Lorsque, loin de chez soi, le cœur gros, on s'enfuit
L'accent, mais c'est un peu le pays qui vous suit

C'est un peu cet accent, invisible bagage
Le parler de chez soi qu'on emporte en voyage
C'est pour le malheureux à l'exil obligé
Le patois qui déteint sur les mots étrangers
Avoir l'accent enfin, c'est chaque fois qu'on cause
Parler de son pays en parlant d'autre chose

Non, je ne rougis pas de mon si bel accent
Je veux qu'il soit sonore et clair, retentissant
Et m'en aller tout droit, l'humeur toujours pareille
Emportant mon accent sur le coin de l'oreille

Mon accent, il faudrait l'écouter à genoux
Il vous fait emporter la Provence avec vous
Et faire chanter sa voix dans tous nos bavardages
Comme chante la mer au fond des coquillages

Écoutez, en parlant je plante le décor
Du torride Midi dans les brumes du Nord
Il évoque à la fois le feuillage bleu-gris
De nos chers oliviers aux vieux troncs rabougris
Et le petit village à la treille splendide
Éclabousse de bleu la blancheur des bastides

Cet accent-là, mistral, cigales et tambourins
À toutes mes chansons donnent un même refrain
Et quand vous l'entendez chanter dans mes paroles
Tous les mots que je dis dansent la farandole.

References

- *Colloquial French* by Alan Moys (Routledge, 1996)

- *Everyday French Idioms* by J.P. Lupson (Nelson Thornes Ltd, 1986)

- *La Vie Outre-Manche*, French-language magazine by Concorde French Language Publications

Acknowledgments

I would like to thank many of my clients who shared their own problems and inspired me to write about them. They include Andy and Janet Busby, Ashley Scott, Fleur Rodway, Gill Moore, Joe Kennedy, Kim Potter, Michael Slipper, Neil Everden, Neil Grant, Tresanna Borgman and David Coombs.

David Coombs even has a really lovely phrase about the French language: "French is an artist's language; if it sounds beautiful, it is correct." So true.

I would also like to thank Chris Payne (http://www.christopherjohnpayne.com) for his help and advice on the making of this book, and his advice and support to authors, as well as Naomi Munts (naomimuntsproofreading.co.uk) for her thorough editing work and Ken Leeder for creating a great cover (www.kenleederdesign.co.uk).

One final thing...

I would really appreciate it if you would review my book on Amazon. Also, if you think I have forgotten something, drop me a line or ask me any question by emailing me at frenchtuition@gmx.co.uk.

And if I have enough requests, who knows, I may write another book or create some videos.

I live in Wiltshire at the moment and I mainly teach clients one-on-one, often via video calls. I also run a French board games evening once a month.

Also written by Nadine Webb: ***Thinking Stories***, a series of short inspirational stories for children and adults alike.

Printed in Great
Britain
by Amazon